half woman half grief

Maya Kalaria

Illustrated by Ellie Coates

First printing: 2020

Illustrations © 2020 by Ellie Coates

Book design © 2020 by Crackle & Pop

ISBN 978 1 5272 6066 5

www.mayakalaria.com

my story

I was terrified about writing this part. Putting it off for weeks, I kept wondering how I was going to explain this book. How could I possibly introduce my heart, my life, and the truest expression of who I am?

And then suddenly it all became clear. This is terrifying, *because* this is my heart, my life, and the truest expression of who I am. That is exactly why I must share it. This is my story, and it has not been easy.

I was born in London in 1986 and grew up with my mum, dad and brother in a few different places before we settled in Barnsley, a small town in the north of England. I was a dreamy yet ambitious child. I had always known that I was a writer, and that my life's goal was to publish a book. I was mystical, tiger-loving and I never hesitated to express what I wanted.

My mother, Nutan, was radiant. Born to a Gujarati family in Kisumu, Kenya, she was beautiful, tall, striking, confident, loving, ferocious and warm. My safe place. My everything. I loved her so very much. She knew me intimately and was an advocate for my wildest dreams. Even at the age of eight, she sent my work to publishers. Admiring her short hair and bold fashion sense, I always used to try her shoes on, quietly lamenting that they were far too big for me. I remember how safe her arms and her presence felt. She was a protection from anything the world could throw at me.

When I was nine, she was admitted to hospital with Leukemia. My brother and I weren't told about the severity of her illness, but my grandparents moved in to look after us. We used to visit her in hospital, playing Scrabble in the waiting room. When we eventually saw her, I remember how she always had her familiar purple tracksuit on, which I loved. I now realise how difficult these visits were for children our age to get our heads around, but we somehow managed to.

On the 5th December, 1996, I had a lift home from school with my friend's mum, as was the usual routine. When I entered the house, I saw my grandmother crying, but thought nothing of it. I asked my dad how mum was, to which he answered that she was OK. Later on that evening, however, my brother and I were doing our homework when dad appeared, told us he wanted to speak to us and disappeared again. My brother, with panic in his voice, asked me if I thought something had happened to mum. This was so beyond my comprehension that I quickly dismissed his remark. There was no way something so terrible could, or should, ever happen to us.

But, as I'm sure you would have guessed by now, the worst had happened. My beloved mother, Nutan Patel, had died that day, in Sheffield Hallam Hospital. And I never got to say goodbye. When my dad broke the news, I just ran to the door and held the handle in shock, saying *no* repeatedly as my world splintered around me.

I wrote a poem for her the next day, in a deep place of shock that would lay dormant in my body for years. When her funeral day came, my brother and I were encouraged to see her, the horror etched upon our faces as we placed our eyes on what was once our smiling mother. I placed the poem in her coffin. The memory of that moment, of seeing her, was forever burned into me. The whole day felt so tragic yet so absurd. We should not have been doing this. This wasn't how things were supposed to be. I was supposed to have my mother. Why would she leave me? Was I not enough for her to stay? How on earth was I supposed to carry on without the one woman who chose to bring me into this world?

In a bittersweet moment of irony, we scattered her ashes on my tenth birthday, in a local park which she had loved. And soon after that, my brother and I left our friends and our schools to move across the country and start our lives again with our grandparents. Little did I know that I would return again that year, after my dad had started a relationship with a school friend's mum. We were to become a blended family.

There is so much more I could tell you, so many layers to the story, so many ways in which I struggled. Things that I didn't even know at the time. That I could never put words to. Even now, as I look back, I still have to unpick the layers of pain from my heart and rake through the trauma held in my body as a silent sum of all the years I became a shadow of myself.

My brother and I were never given the adequate space, time and support to grieve for our mother. This was due to quite a few things. Our society doesn't provide the correct tools to support people through grief and our family did not have the vocabulary nor the emotional capacity to know or give us what we needed. In fact, my father, brother and I didn't talk to each other about her for about 20 years. I became afraid to bring her up in case people thought I should have been over her by now, or I shouldn't dwell on the past. I realise now that this silence had felt to me like a bitter denial of her, of us, of our loss. She was frozen between us, an unspoken love song, a grief unerupted. I thought this was normal at the time and tried to 'get on with things' as I was expected to. But without her protection, I had no-one to sufficiently guide me through the storm that was to be the rest of my life. Through latent racism, bullying, self-hatred, isolation and a severe difficulty in both familial and romantic relationships.

I felt like I was running a race with my peers, only that someone had shot me in the leg with an invisible bullet. The wound, therefore, was invisible. And I had learned to keep it that way for fear of falling apart, of cracking open, or being seen as too much, too sensitive, or too weak. I was limping my way through life, comparing myself to other people in the race and wondering why I was never as excited or happy or as confident in myself as they seemed to be. My unspoken grief had become so deeply embedded within me that it had buried my personality underneath a series of elaborate coping mechanisms and a deeply unhealed trauma. I had become painfully shy, self-conscious and perfectly controlled. Or so I thought.

The poems you are about to read were my unravelling. They were my surrender, my excavation and my resurrection. They were written over a period of four years. After seven years of not writing, and during a particularly difficult relationship, I picked up my pen again. I didn't know what would come out, but I knew something needed to. None of the poems were planned, and all were given to me as intuitive downloads; a felt sense that somehow translated onto the page. Even now, I can't remember how they were formed. I was often woken up in the early hours of the morning to write down a sudden flash of inspiration.

They came to me in a non-linear way. Sometimes I wrote about the initial stages of grief, and sometimes I wrote about spiritual lessons I had learned along the way. When I was putting this book together, however, I clearly saw that they had effortlessly mapped out my own journey into the underworld; my descent, initiation and ascent. My own heroic journey.

Like most women, the darkness was not something I was ever encouraged to embrace within myself. The rage I had accumulated over the years of silence, however, was raw and overwhelming. I needed to express it, to get it out of my body, and for it to be witnessed by others. Love and light is all very well, but what would I do with my rage, my shame, my despair, my guttural sobs, my desperate sadness? Through the journey of writing my poetry, I met the dark feminine, and started re-membering her essence within me. I wanted her dark archetypal symbols to saturate the book as a sacred testament to what has long been forgotten in our collective psyche. Through her unwavering guidance, I learned what it was like to love myself again; the scared, vulnerable, broken, resentful, raging parts that I had dissociated from for so long. The four chapters of this book represent the different stages I went through with my grief; the initial shock, the descent into my own sorrow, the meeting of my shadow within the darkness and the re-emergence back into the light, this time hand-in-hand with the dark feminine.

There were other factors which helped me to heal, too. I started meditating around the time of writing these poems, and connecting with my intuition was incredibly powerful. The support of my friends was key, especially their celebration of my authenticity. Therapy, both holistic and conventional, provided a safe place for me to coax back the parts of me which had long been hidden in terror. Sharing the true impact of all the years of silent grief with my family was a huge catharsis. And finding love again with someone who had met me as a passionate, sensitive, ferocious poet and continued to love me as that woman enabled me to peel away everything that was not me, until I reached the core of who I really was.

This book is for anyone who has experienced grief of any kind; personal, colonial, collective, environmental, and everything in between. We experience grief on a regular basis, and those tiny losses can create hundreds of papercuts within us that, if left unattended to, leave gaping wounds. I want you to know that you are not alone. That there are others out there who have also experienced the earth-shattering agony of grief. That hope, joy and healing are still possible, no matter how hard it may be to imagine it at the time.

And, last but not least, this book is for my mother. The woman who birthed me. Birthed love through love. Without you, I wouldn't exist. Without you, this wouldn't be possible. Thank you for your love; for your undying confidence in your young, wild, tender daughter. Thank you for seeing the beauty in my everything. Because you saw me, I now truly see myself.

This is a testament of my love for you, for myself, and for everyone who is reading this book.

twenty years clawing out
of your coffin. resurrecting
myself from dust
to crawl through mud
on bloody hands and knees.
screaming the night air right
out of my lungs. howling
at the moon with
streaming tears and
thirsty sobs.
unchaining my domesticated
soul. setting her free.
baring my teeth. eyes
widened in anger.
i now stand here
with dirt in my fingernails
and your pride in my heart.

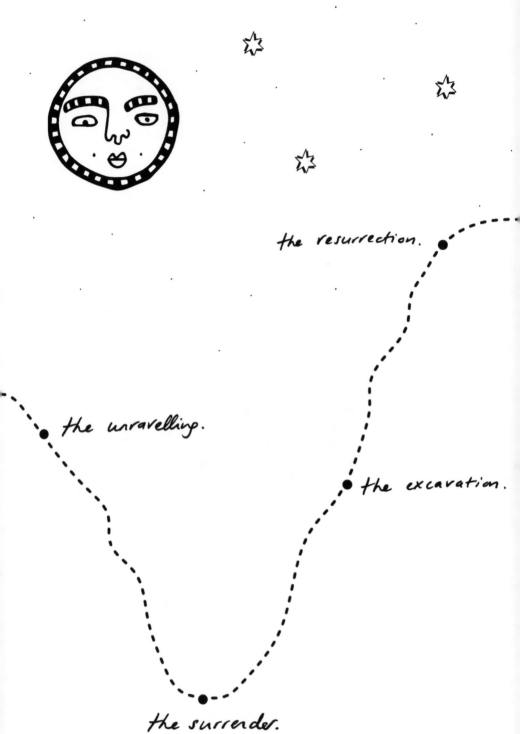

the resurrection.

the unravelling.

the excavation.

the surrender.

the unravelling.

the unravelling .

and such is the
boundless fury of my
pain. brushed off by
denial. tiny yet dense
within me, each grain of dismissal
impossible to grasp. to extract
from these limbs.
wordless. soundless. except for
the way my whole body
aches and convulses and responds
to this world. silently.
except for every breath within me.
every longing i hold inside.
every terror i hold dear. yes,
such is the boundless
fury of my pain.
that telling you wasn't,
isn't enough.
that now i must tell
the whole world.

for every moment
i do not say
i am sad
it creeps a little
further
into my bones
and nestles
itself right there.

the unravelling.

years of unspent
grief.
she crouches in me
silently.
awaiting her
turn.
a currency.
she readies herself
to jump.
my throat
tightens.

the unravelling .

come out of my heart.
resurrect from
dust.
tell me you love me one last time.
stroke my hair.
please don't let this be it.
i don't think i can take you not
being
here.
i was someone with you
that i will never be
with anyone.

once there was a spider
who was big enough to eat birds. it lived
in the rainforest in brazil.
it crawled across our
tv screen as i lay my head on
your lap. i was ill, and you sat there
stroking my hair and feeding me
cold coke through a straw.
i think of that day whenever i think of you
and even when i don't. i think of that day and
how you loved me and how that was all i could taste.
i think of how i may never know that
love again and how exquisite the pain is
that bubbles up inside me. just like the coke
i sipped from the cup in your hand.

you are
ground
into the
marrow
of my bones.

how ironic
that it was
the very thing
that
ended you.

ashes to ashes.
i set my idea of you
alight

and set you adrift on the river.

my ten year old self
screams
and runs after you.

she has been here
before.

the unravelling.

the unravelling.

you live between my ribs.
in the tightest of
places
i enclose you.

my bones ache with every
day
i do not let
you out.

i feel dizzy
with
missing
you.

i can't hear
for my sobs.

there was grief in my lungs
(he said).
there was nothing i could do.
i had taken a big hit as a small child
(he said).
it was irreversible. finito.
damage done.
i didn't ask for this
(i said).
but now there is less air because
she's gone.
she took my ability to breathe
with her when she took her last
breath
(i thought).
because some things are always better
left unsaid.

my heart
beats inwards
at the thought
of you.
for a moment,
it does a double-take.
for a moment,
it forgets you
are only
a memory.
it longs for
you
in the
loneliest
of places.

the unravelling.

in the cemetery, three people met, bound by death's softly spoken hymn.

death's husband.
  death's daughter.
    death's son.

      waiting silently
      beneath
      the willow trees.

a large grey house
exists somewhere
in my
sadness.
and it is strange.
and it is familiar.

there comes a moment.
if you have lost,
you'll know the one.

it's that split second
where
you are changed
on a cellular level.

as your confused heart
accepts
it's eternal weight.

and their absence
bumps into you in   room.
                    every

no more grasping
onto
things.
no more
covering up.
denying.
lying.
no.
i lost you.
i lost.
i lost.
i lost.

the unravelling.

the unravelling .

there is a vast space within me which i have
known before, which i have tried to fill. but
today i could not help but hear my echoes within
it. the moon reflected on a lotus leaf, as though
that was all that ever was, and ever will be. a
stillness in which i at first wanted to scream
and cry in grief, as i knew nothing mattered,
nothing or no-one. it is all an illusion. a grand
illusion. the emptiness i had always known was
there had come back to show itself to me, and
i could not escape it this time. the black velvet
dress i wore to my mother's funeral. the flower
tied around my plait. i knew it was there all
along, and i had been running because it was too
eternal, and too huge, and too empty. knowing it
made everything seem so insignificant. nothing
mattered.

and yet it all did.

the surrender.

the surrender.

spinning.
head
throbbing.
i danced
for rain
which
never fell.
clouds
withdrew
and all
i had
was me,
bare feet
on barren
ground.
i walked.

you told me to stop crying
because it would upset them.
and i did. and i understood
that you could not handle
my despair but this was
not the time for that.
i, too, needed to feel
all of it right then
and there. and
this belief.
this is
why i
held
my
self
in
at
all
times.

this

       is how

              my sorrow

                    turned inwards.

it's ok.
carry it to the river
if you must.
and if you must,
shed.
shed as many layers
as you need to.
and if you must,
weep.
do not stop your
tears from
falling.

and
what else can i do
when you
continue to crash
through me?

it is
my fate
to be brought to
my knees at your
every command.

i have always been
half woman
half grief.

the surrender.

you are so beautiful in your pain.
the way you hold your pain
with such dignity.
the way you move with your pain.
the way it tightens your stomach and
twists it into knots
yet you still breathe.
the way the knife still lies
inside you
yet you still wake up.
the way you form yourself around it
so tenderly. so bravely.
as if you're so in love with
your wound
that you do not wish to disturb it.
oh you tender
vulnerable
broken
brave
creature.

how beautiful
it is
not
to smile.
how exquisite
it is
to look at you
darkly. directly.
and tell you
the truth of my
experience.

when the dimming light
barely hits the water.
that is my time.
when the clouds
loom over
the sky
my heart soars.
i breathe so easily in
this dying light.
i empty the heavy contents
of my heart
into the fading
whispers
of the stream.
she transports it
to a place
beyond words.

there will always
be a part of me
you do
not know.

the surrender.

why do you not feel the joy
of love?
you ask.

i answer you.

i first knew love
by its absence.

how could my love
endure such a
birth
and still look like love.
still feel like love.

when love shares its heartbeat
with fear
it is a
different creature
entirely.

the surrender.

i dug a grave
inside myself
and buried
you in there.
i carved
your name
so deeply
into my heart
that i became
your living
breathing
memory.

i will carry my broken heart into the desert

cradled through lands of bleak
nothingness,
with not a soul or barren tree in sight.
there will be no more illusions,
no mirage.
i will ride into sandstorms with my
eyes wide open,
just to lay under the midnight sky and
bury my heart in warm dunes,
listening to its faint drum beating
in the stillness.
just to witness the stars playing hide and seek
with this, my most beloved treasure.
and upon the light of dawn,
upon awakening,
just to rise and hear it beating
a little bit stronger.

the excavation.

the excavation.

ride
through the
endless tunnels
and meet me
in here.
in darkness.
hear me in
the shadows.
feed me black
roses through
the bars.
we will pick
pomegranates
together.
you know
i am the
one you are
afraid of.

the tenuous line between the land
of the breathing
and the realm of ghosts.
thin as thread.
silken. slips through a needle
easily.
i live
in a place
where each world seeps through
the seams.
where death exists
even
in the living.

you
shot the stars out of
the sky.
taught me how
to find
light
in the darkness.

taught me to say
my own name
clearly.
to straighten my spine
into a warrior's.
showed me love
didn't have to be
gentle
to be right.
caressed me
fiercely.
knowingly.
smothered me with
the truth.
blessed my rage.

you
loved me
from the shadows.
nourished me
with death.
taught me to raise
my voice from a
whisper
to a
growl.

the excavation.

i walk towards you in the dark
because i know i can see.
i do not need light.
i need no hands to feel you.
you are within and without me.
your sound is my beloved
and your voice hums my name.
my eyes remain open.
dense. tender.
the giver of death.
the taker of life.
i trust your rhythm as i trust
my own heartbeat.
a child born from darkness
does not need a map home.

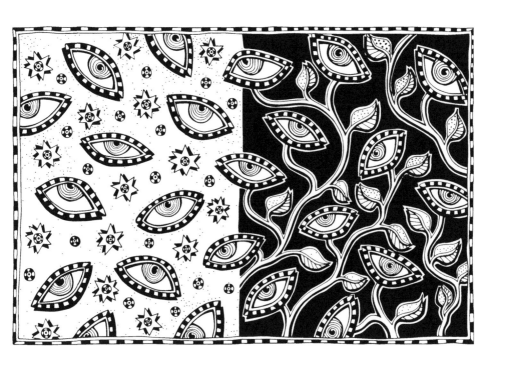

did you know?
did we know?
did we decide on this
back when we were
formless,
before we had even
taken shape?
did we know that
you would leave
for me to become this,
to question the
heavens and earth
so vehemently,
to rise with such
ferocity
above the pain
you left behind
in your wake,
in your ashes?

did you know
i would grip
my pen just a little
bit tighter
without you?
that i could only
grow as i
clutched at your
startling
absence?
did we collude
in the unseen realms,
did we conspire
like two teenage girls
as we planned
our lives,
your death,
together?

i am crying when you find me. you pick me up
and look deeply into me, your eyes full of fierce
love. and you tell me i am beautiful, and kind, and
intelligent, and ferocious, and wanted, and loved so
very deeply, so eternally. so unconditionally. you tell
me that it is they who are broken, not me. you take
my hand and tell me that we will get through this
together, that i will never want for anything again
because you are here to stay. you will remind me
every day of this, so that i never forget. you stroke
my hair as i fall asleep, knowing you will be there
when i awake. you tell me that i will grow into the
most amazing woman, full of vision and purpose,
and that i can't even imagine the magnitude of what
i will achieve. you softly push my hair behind my
ears, kiss my forehead and whisper, oh-so-gently,
hold on sweetheart, just you wait.

i love you as two women would. as i would
but more.
as i would but with the force of
another,
the one whose voice creaks inside these
bones,
whose honeyed laughter rips through these scars.
the one who birthed me. birthed
love through love.
her blood competes with mine to race
through arteries
and flood blue veins.
her long hands grip these slim wrists, each pose
in her possession, each breath of mine
her expression of what it means to be alive.
and so her heart is mine. and so
her love is mine to give.
and so i can only ever love you
as two women would.

the excavation.

the excavation.

i exist in your absence
but
i wanted to see me. so
laid out on solid ground, i
drew a line of chalk
around myself.
examined me. looked at
the shape of me.
until the rains came, that is.
all trace of me washed away
just like that.
just
like that.

on hands and knees,
sodden.
i scrambled for chalk,
for paint,
for a goddamn stone just to
see myself again.
i did. and i was different
this time. and only two things
became certain.

the earth.
and the rain.

the earth.
and the rain.

i wrote myself
awake.
letting the pen
bleed
in places
i could not.

honour her.

honour her.

you will never be that version
of yourself again.

but before you lower her
into her grave

make sure she damn well didn't
die in vain.

the excavation.

the resurrection.

the resurrection.

thank you pain.
you're trying to tell me what happened.
you're trying to articulate
without words
what i endured.
how you were just
broken shards in my tight knuckles.
how i clutched you
until my hands bled.
how every movement hurt.
sorrow.
rage.
betrayal.
how they lit fires within me which
burned so brightly that
somehow
they transformed you
into diamond.

let me
bathe.
let me
stain.
in the
dark
cherry wine.
the blood red
of all
that
i am.

and
as it broke
to reveal the most
tender of spaces

even more love
crept in.

as i bent down
to pick up the
parts of me
i had
discarded,
i grieved for the
years
i had walked this earth
un-whole.

it happened.
my heart finally
split
into two.

and who knew
such
joy
could be found
on the edge of a
sword.

speak your
unspeakable
to me.
shake the
earth
within.
set fire
to these eyes.
my dams
will burst
for you.

i have been preparing
for this moment.
i have been clearing my throat.
warming my voice.

humming.

chanting.

weeping.

screaming.

for precisely this moment.

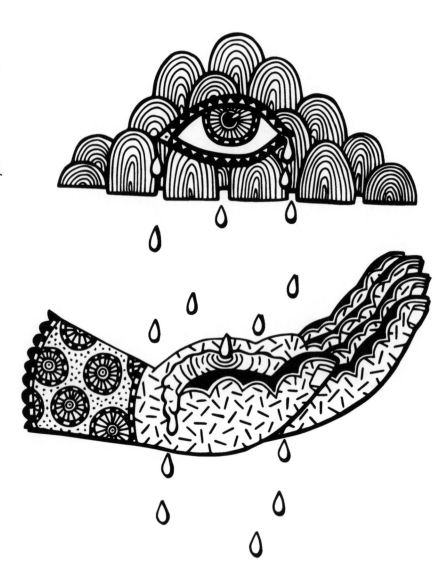

these are not new tears.
mourn with me.
wear black. wear white.
these are not new tears.
they once fell from you
and me and drained down
through the streets.
into sewers. into rivers.
oceans. mourn with me.
they sat there, sedentary.
perfectly covered by the
darkness. until it was time.
mourn with me.
it's time for old rain
to fall down new faces.

this is the stuff that shakes you.
makes you shiver. scream. sob.

rocks you to your core
and then keeps coming back for more.
this is what rips a person-shaped hole
from your life and makes you question
who you are.

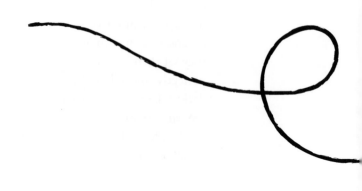

this is what gives life its meaning and
takes it all away.

this is the poison and its antidote.
visceral, raw love in its purest state.
this is the heavy ache of our soul as it
grows beyond what we ever
thought we knew.

this is grief.
the most beautiful, ruthless beast.

the resurrection.

what is love?
she asked.

like a whisper,
the answer came.

it is to give birth.
it is to be born.
and it is to die
all at once.

L - #0375 - 080321 - C0 - 229/152/4 - PB - DID3038129